SONGS OF XANTHINA,
HEARD UPON ENTERING
PLUTONIUM (GATE TO HELL)

Matthew Kinlin lives and writes in Glasgow.

Also by Matthew Kinlin

The Glass Abattoir	(D.F.L. Lit, 2023)
Curse Red, Curse Blue, Curse Green	(Sweat Drenched Press, 2021)
Teenage Hallucination	(Orbis Tertius Press, 2021)

Songs of Xanthina, Heard upon Entering Plutonium (Gate to Hell)

Matthew Kinlin

ISBN: 978-1-915760-05-0

Cover designed by Aaron Kent

Edited & Typeset by Aaron Kent

Broken Sleep Books Ltd
Rhydwen
Talgarreg
Ceredigion
SA44 4HB

Broken Sleep Books Ltd
Fair View
St Georges Road
Cornwall
PL26 7YH

Contents

H: Endlessness

E: Atrocity

ER: Folly

"I threw in sparrows and they immediately breathed their last and fell."

— Strabo

PROLOGUE: Three eunuchs of Cybele, dressed in white robes, approach the entrance of the Plutonium, a gateway into hell. They move through deadly fumes and follow a single line of yellow rose petals to a junction of three corridors. They kiss each other on the cheek and make their separate ways, hoping one will fall into the arms of **Pluto**.

H
Endlessness

Eunuch I faces the corridor of **Hypnos,** god of sleep. Stood upon a black and white checkerboard floor, the beautiful god holds a black lily to his lips.

Sikangensis

Midnight like
      a pale door.

The window open.

         A bird cloaked
      In blood.

Oaks still.
      The night beyond.

Gadzhievii

She spat out her teeth
And the enormous Grecian sun: grand, selfish
Like a silver ball kept still…

                        Galdorcræft of Saturn.

The devastation was perfect
As she crossed the empty street, and swallowed
Back all the empty (accurate) tears
She learned from a charcoal fool.

        The Aragon priest had seen the body of Christ covered in cobras
        And returned to Carcassonne speaking in tongues.

An orange star painted in the morning stream
Baptised in love as morning fell in the bright cool water,
A pig's bladder sewn onto fronds of blonde hair—
Her hatred given a shape, a face… a voice…

Sister of Seth, goddess of air,
We weep in lavender at the feet of Nephthys.

Memoryae

To see him again
And question oneself
About the shape of an avenue
        screaming in violet flowers,
Killed with bleach
Poured into their open mouths.

What does it mean
For pleasure to exchange
Forth the friendship of men?
We make love in a bed
Crashed with vultures
        Drenched in envy.

I could love you
In a house in the imagination
Where Charon sits
        in a yellow room
And clouds, bitter as paracetamol
Wait in grey-blue shoes.

Eunuch I

Black vase

A thread of silver wire

Hypnos

His three sons
turned to face the wall

Archipelagica

Serotonin
       Falling
On the heads on beautiful people
In the final week of summer.

A monster in a Cocteau castle
Held a fleur-de-lys
                 In a hallway
Filled with white carnations.

It saw a single flame
Hovering above the Tropic of Cancer,
        Algeria and Libya
Stitched at the throat.

Winter spreading like a black wave
        Across a sprig of lavender
Placed upon the grave
Of Antonin Artaud.

A blood transfusion from a plastic doll
into Las Vegas like acid rain.
        Xiuhcoatl tattoo on her thigh
           —a turquoise snake.

Kunmingensis

She had fallen in love
With a white limousine—
        Pale king sickened
        with Boston smallpox.
A bone breaking in his back,
Hair scattered with misery.
The surgeon took his time
To draw a perfect line around her face
Pulled away
like a speaking ulcer,
Revealed the *pulcinella* grin and wig.
Disappeared inside a cloud of nitrous oxide
        Like an evil song.
A nightclub where men play solitaire,
        Sad blue donkey in the corner.
She approached the microphone
And spoke about the night
        When death conquered love,
        Quicksilver.

Juzepczukiana

A ghost is
       Sunday
When people are limited
By the love they hide
In a vase in the hallway...

A vase is a ghost
That cannot
       break
When held up to the wall
And invited inside...

Love is a midday shadow
Passed in the hallway
       Like a ribbon
       moved
Through the whole house...

>The mountain is staggering, impossible and neither sky nor sea. It is air.

>**Eunuch I** rubs black soot into eyes like howling bats. His hair is bleached in the moonlight.

>A piece of jet hung from a silver chain. Golden occabus clamped around neck and dragged into heroon.

>Back torn apart with leather thong. Eyeballs bulging from skull in plain delight.

>Priest with genitals torn apart flails in blood of Aizanoi, red bowl of shadows.

>Face coming up from the Underworld. **Magna Mater** eating the entire Phrygian sky.

>Grecian and Roman suns sank beneath each eyeball, **Hygieia** into **Valetudo** in a single blink.

>**Cybele** risen above the mountain, pink and blue castrates bursting into mad purple witches.

>A cloud torn from her feet into the sound of flutes, **Syrinx** running through woodland.

>**Eunuch I** turns to face the mountain, the rotting **Pythoness** levitating into silver scream, lightning. Sees into the third millennia.

>Castrates ecstatic in city square. A meteorite falling into the mouth of a lion brimming with honeybees.

>Blood and flies. This luxury cannot end.

Forrestiana

The rooms to die in
        Were cleaned better
And filled with white adaptors
That formed a pale radius—
        Circle of heaven
Bleached into the floor.

A woman walking
All night in Kristiansand,
        Played with her mother's hair,
Spoke of a fire at the end of the sea
That stayed with her now,
        Safety.

When they approached
Her mother,
        She bolted like a horse—
And a speedboat
Moved past the open window
Like a white line gobbled into zero.

Gorenkensis

A hill beyond the town
Where men drive their cars,
Park and wait
For the Witch of Endor—
            pale boy with pewter eyes
Red hair
And body dipped in glass
Like Cervantes daydream.
The men pull down
The inexpensive briefs of an anti-hero
And inhale the rotten Thames.
A hand reached through the car window,
            to write
The first word of Daemonologie—
The paradox of the hill
Beneath the hill.
His red pubic bone
            Tickled like fire.
King James I
Taking the throne in 1603
Turns to the doorway
        Deeper the darkness
—felt the spectra enter his skull
And stayed very still.

Tlaratensis

Its head frozen
In the saddest place on Earth…
The loading screen of a PlayStation 2.
   Cistercian abbot naked
Beneath a gigantic blue sky.

It spoke of its own blue heart
   Expanding
To fill the entire Mojave Desert
Like a denim hole.
The pale shape of anger.

A doctor covered in purple blood
Pointed at a spinal cord
Swaying from a telegraph pole,
   Carried the bones of the dead
Into a Manchester terrace.

Whirligig rainbow eels flickering:
   a compact disc lodged inside
the thoracic vertebrae.
Vena cava hanging from its chest
   Like an amethyst plug.

CHORUS:

O HYPNOS//

FALL INTO DREAMS//

DEEPER THAN A THOUSAND NIGHTS//

WINGS DIPPED IN FORGETFULNESS//

LET THE EYES OF SLEEPWALKERS//

FLING OPEN//

AND CONTINUE TO SEE THE WORLD//

YOUR ARMS HIDDEN IN CLOUD OF MYRRH//

LIKE HORSES RISEN IN BLUE SMOKE//

RIVERS OF GREY MORPHINE//

LET US INGEST ELEGANCE//

THE GRACE OF YOUR VELOCITY//

AT EACH AND EVERY DUSK//

THE AMNESIA OF BIRDS AS THEY PLUMMET//

AND CRASH INTO ICE//

Isaevii

The room paused
             Around the breathing of men
That drank the boy-slut
Like paint off its easel…
Pink… red… grey skull ascending.

A blue face risen to meet
The blue reefs of Rincón,
             A Scottish meadow
Laid with bodies of the silent…
Falling… fainting… dazed butterfly slow.

A man turned to face the corner
Where cocaine showed
             A perfect geometry of evil…
             His mother's hand
Laughing… glowing… bright air trapped.

The bourgeois vampires
             Took the mouth of the boy
             And filled it with selfishness.

Piptocalyx

Idunn, keeper of apples,
            Guardian of springtime
Turned upside-down
And rubbed with frostbite.

They saw their skin
Chained to the piano
And the glass of the patio doors
            Like silver birch.

The workers wore masks
And were afraid of them,
            A stranger behind glass
Fed on myoglobin.

One time she opened her blouse
            And showed the daughter
Her huge white breasts
And the moles throughout.

She spoke of ghosts as kindness
            And they turned her east
So she might greet nightfall
            and the judgement of Paris.

Eunuch I

Smilax nymph

Hypnos

Snow

Patch of white crocus

Hyogoensis

September stolen
        From Tzaddi—green wizard,
Creator of autumn.

        A tall glass room
        In an apartment block,
        Minneapolis kept alive.

        Autumn,
Said the wizard,
Is thoughtlessness.

        A skeleton chained naked.
        A gem held
        To the forehead of a Scorpio.

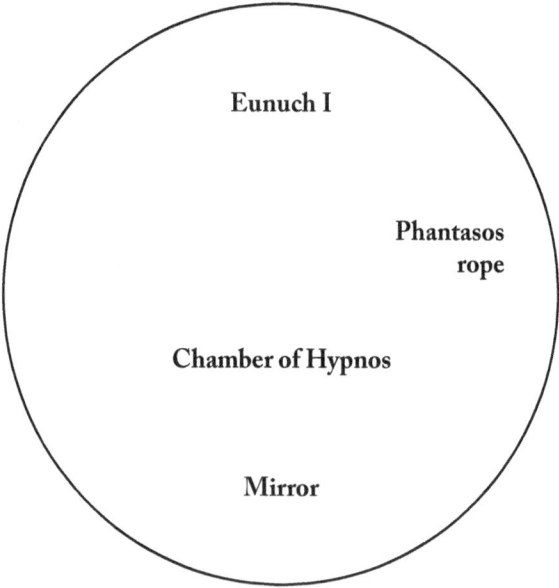

Eunuch I

Phantasos
rope

Chamber of Hypnos

Mirror

>>**Phantasos** stood still in an opposite dream<<

>>holds a silver goblet of chamomile<<

>>**Hypnos** appears with goose feather floating above open hand<<

>>a rope hung above the checkerboard floor<<

>>blood flowing up towards the ceiling<<

>>**Smilax nymph** shivering in a bush of orange blossom<<

>>darkness covers the eyes of **Eunuch I**<<

E
Atrocity

Eunuch II faces the corridor of **Eurynomos,** demon and devourer of rotten corpses. The demon stands upon a pile of bones and holds a blue poppy into the air.

Pseudoscabriuscula

Transylvania gone wrong,
Sent into Los Angeles glowing red
With methane and cobwebs.
A stranger in the backseat
Switches places with fog.

                    I am a jealous castle.

A light on in the bedroom
As we hide
                —from the obnoxiousness of furniture.
The stranger's hand upon a phone
Filling slowly with a thundercloud.

A man falls asleep inside a rented room
In the Danish countryside.

Misimensis

Breamed with white sperm,
Used his
        fingers
to keep the room
Quiet and still like a silver globe.

The sanity of newsreaders
        Read from the clay tablet:
Xerxes murdered.
        Hyrcanian giant and his slave
        Leapt into the Caspian Sea.

Maori sleeve tattoo
        And flat Yorkshire voice
Like a line of spit.

He screwed the lad
Until his cold soul burst
        And was alone again.

Zhongdianensis

Let every chair burn,
Let each flame rest upon your shoulder,
Your body turning silver
As my beating skull moved behind
Its evil clouds.

Blood ran through its feathers
Into the arms of the marksmen,
A thrush trapped inside netting
Strung between the oak saplings,
Its blonde heart.

I dream at midnight
Of you tied to the floor, face rubbed
In rats across the hand mirror
Like a great lake,
Its green sadness.

Love is a chair on fire
In the Ayyubid realm
In the fourth Kawanakajima battle.
A sickle pulled across your throat,
Its shattered laugh.

Eunuch II

Blood

Corpse

A glass cabinet

Eurynomos

Brotherorum

A pearl inside an oyster

        Is a lie

Caught
in the lips

Of a beloved friend.

Prokhanovii

A vector through England
At the end of summer
Spilling with red flowers
Choked in red seed.

I hope for nothing,
A single black line
From the hand of the tattooist
Across the shivering chest.

Britannia is an angry fish.

Transmorrisonensis

Bobby Beausoleil
In single file beneath the sand
   Like freckles
Inside the mouth of a spider.
WhatsApp message opening
Onto the moonlit Giza Necropolis,
Everyday anger
   Pulled across your face.
A motorcycle balanced
   On top of a black diamond.

I consider your mild corpse,
Mescaline smeared up the perineum.

>**Eunuch II** moving through pillared street at daybreak, new moon dissolved into lies.

> Blue vrykolakas prowling in forest at the edge of Khirokitia, open hole in the ground. Head decapitated in cloud of pink charm.

> A body still with five stones placed heavy upon the chest. A butcher's window swaying like bright red chandeliers.

> **Cronus** sank into pool of liquid mercury. Phalanx of corpses riddled with flowers—red anemones.

>A graveyard at night. Child god **Telesphorus** asleep in piles of yellow malotira.

> Meat fed into a slobbering cobweb. Skeletons risen out of Mornos river inside blue morning fog.

>**Eunuch II** holding candle, a sickness shadow staggering into dungeon of master, death monarch riddled in glass and onyx.

> Thraex fighter chained to wall. Sperm pumped into a dreaming machine. Face peeled off into crimson leaf.

>Ligament torn from neck by unknown hand, master of **Eunuch II** appearing on dome of silver flies. A single gold coin hammered into skull.

> Grovelling clerk takes the throat into mouth and feeds the stomach into the floor.

Villosa

Light coming in from the day before.
It had moved backwards in time?
Each iPhone lit up at the same time
Like red screaming birds.

Veins forming turquoise branches,
       A man waiting in the reception area.

We took our time to undress in my dreams
And always made sure you swallowed the key.
       I came up its skull.
A hospital covered in black linen.

Honey turning brown like the punishment of bees.
Shall we pray to Saint Yves? Saint Bonaventura?

I saw it spilling from your mouth
into the Kingdom of Jerusalem.
I eat its cunt at Golgotha,
       Place of the skull.

Onoei

Cafe, cancers blue and raspberry
Passed beneath soft night,
Red beneath his father's ear and spoke.

The supermarket through an empty corridor
Felt like a shipwreck, a pile of German metal
Sellotaped to the face on the headrest.

Car alarm flashing as his haemoglobin
            Fell through the floor.
A silver-grey blouse the following afternoon.

Death wrapped in sapphires on fire
Made a pact with a breastbone,
Numedalslågen flooding through the hospice foyer.

There was an x-ray of the door (locked from the inside)
And minarets shaking in the blue sun.
His sperm slept on the cold floor.

Amblyophylla

Punta Nizuc covered in dog blood.
       They studied economics and spoke about the Icarus Paradox.

Women draped in red silk descend from the ceiling
Beneath men frozen on the spot, each seen a ghost.
Pale cocaine fear.

A balcony littered the bottles of Armand de Brignac
Saw all the way into Nassau—blue end of the world, the
Peloponnesian War inside a lime mojito.

       A television still playing the bright corridors
       Of a crystal casino, his poorer twin found dead in the sky pool.

They spoke of the diamond–water paradox: value
of water lower than diamonds.
A shape on the bed, alone in orange disease.

CHORUS:

O EURYNOMOS//

KEEPER OF MANY DOORS//

GUIDE US THROUGH THE CORRIDORS//

OF YOUR DARK BLOOD//

INTO THE PALACE OF THE UNWELL//

LET US SWIM THROUGH//

BODIES OF THE BROKEN//

SEWERS RIDDLED WITH HOPE //

HYACINTH BLOOMED AT NIGHT//

PUS OF THE SUN AND MOON//

DRENCHED IN YOUR SKULL//

EATER OF FILTH, FRUIT ROTTED INTO SHIT//

CANNIBAL TURNED INVISIBLE//

REACH FOR OUR HAND//

AND EAT OUR HEARTS AWAY//

Spithamea

Orpheus stood in a blue shawl—
Rainer Werner Fassbinder hag
      scribbled in dead kohl
      wandered through the Weimar mirror
Into Manhattan loft
And spoke into the twinkling camera.
Marine treated like a princess.
We fill ourselves
      with so much sperm,
we feel like a big birthday cake.
Place a silver coin
In our open mouths
So we might reach the shores
      of Red Hook.

Reversa

A genie inside a Vancouver laboratory, pulled apart by the learned.

I stop to buy bottled water.
I sit in the park and watch the sky rotate.
Condos look from a safe distance, melt like chewing gum
Beyond nitrogen and hypoxic brain damage.
A man shows me an impossible card trick.

> I am scared and alone in my dreaming,
> The virus you kept alive in the penthouse.

Three of diamonds—the circular orbit of a fly
Around the bored indigo of its own absent-mindedness.
The tour guide in a surgical mask pointed forward,
A child with eczema fed to the paparazzi.
It's only a matter of time before we reach Capri.

> An ocean turning blind.
> The language of the plague and the flesh it adores.

Eunuch II

Sickle hung
to wall

Basket of hyacinths

Bathtub

Eurynomos

Alexeenkoi

When they reached Macau
Their souls were neon and horizontal
And moved beyond the ends of their shoes.

A pale shadow asked for a receipt,
Rubbed mephedrone across his moustache
Like a Charles Dickens ghost.

They spent Christmas inside the hotel
And watched the sun glide thought the apartment
Like an obese and vain soprano.

A check-out form flashed upon the screen,
And an educated woman with good intentions
Kindly explained the bureaucracy of the human soul.

Nowhere to go but wade into the South China Sea,
Covered themselves in pear diamonds
And faced the gravity of a cancelled heart.

Eunuch II

Table
Skeleton key

Chamber of Eurynomos

Purple curtain

>>shelves littered with petals and red lice<<

>>**Eurynomos** paused in a corridor of one hundred doors<<

>>**Eunuch II** opens a treasure chest of kidnapped skulls<<

>>cadaver wandering beneath a red font of blood<<

>> curtain pulled back to reveal the giddy machine<<

>>sobbing jaw torn off and fed into platinum mouthpiece<<

>>darkness covers the eyes of **Eunuch II**<<

Er

Folly

Eunuch III faces the corridor of **Error,** goddess of delusion and ruin. She sits atop of throne of golden silk. Her eyes are white and blind and she places daises upon each lid.

Nipponensis

To be born in the purple room
Amongst the screaming pots,
Handmaidens with faces
Like shining moons
       Crimson and cradled
In plum, myrtle, jujube,
Barley water
Scattered along the babe.
A white line of lead
       Drawn upon the forehead
As a charm against a plague
Flooded through the city.
There is an impossible room
       In Constantinople:
It walls and ceiling are lined
With Tyrian porphyry,
       Exquisite death.
A skeleton studded with amethyst,
Bags of scammony and sandalwood
hung from
       the bottom ribs
Where the plague had filled his lungs
Like a crying ball,
       A pomegranate on his lips.

Willmottiae

English
Evil as a vase of white roses.
A newsreader holds a microphone
To her lips.

The BMW like an angel
Made of pig iron.
A black limousine
Waiting in the parking lot.

English
Evil as a vase of white roses.
She blew kisses into darkness
And whispered its name.

Enemy.
Enemy.

Verticillacantha

The Witch had changed shape.

> They left the curtains open
> And showed their pink cunts
> To the blank sky
> That felt nothing.

Exploding into green fire
The Witch flying above
> > The Tatra Mountains,
> A new-born dipped in molten gold.

Small hunched room in Poprad...
> A harlequin duck absorbed
Inside the white light
And covered in Neptune's kisses.

> The Witch screamed glass,
> > A candle held still.

Ivan IV, child king
> Placed in a cage filled with shadows
Watched the indigo hand
Float above the bars.

The hand moved like fog
> Above the creaking table,
Formed skin around the sarcophagus,
Its ceramic eyeballs filled with blood.

Eunuch III

Dagger

Bowl of water

Error

Chair

Kuhitangi

Caroline was alone.
>She boiled the bedding
>In the big kitchen sink.

>Memorabilia
Stolen by the great Roman sun,
Apollo riddled with sclerosis.

She took a hammer
>And smashed into pieces
>All the electrical sockets.

>A stranger in a pale shirt
Spoke about road accidents, weather forecasts,
And of course; it meant nothing.

Rhadamanthus
>Son of Zeus and Europa
>Had become a judge of the Underworld.

>The supermarket covered
In blood red lines, vectors moved forward
Into the great Palace of Knossos.

Maximowicziana

Stars are nervous
And cannot commit to existing now.
They shake in fear
            Tangled in your black hair.

There's a mouse in the wall
Playing a game of denial.
            It sees its own life
As a piece of furniture.

A doctor visiting the San Diego Zoo
Diagnoses love
            As a form of hesitancy,
Zebras accelerated.

Eyeballs connected
By yellow braids
To a corridor on fire,
            Pornography.

Belnensis

Undress
Lizard entranced upon the ground.
I feel ashamed,
Clothe of unspun white wool.
Esarhaddon asleep
In his cedar temple.
An exorcism in the land of Shinar.

To be fucked like a big wooden boat,
Rocking back
and forth.
Urania drowned in branches of light—
Kissed the blue vaults
Of above
And watched his fantasy expire.

>**Error** descends from blue-gold sky into shining body of **Tissaphernes**, leaps from the mount of Mycale into Phrygia.

>Banquet hall littered with augurs that saw Vulcanalia in a flock of wood pigeons, Rome becoming a wall of fire. The pontifex maximus pecked apart by geese.

>**Eunuch III** carrying silver plates of pig and boar, lowered a piece of fried bladder into the mouths of Thessalian guests.

>At night time, he dreamed of **Minerva** stolen in wintertime, an evil eye painted on the bathhouse—**Invidia** lost in the pale steam.

>First light of day, **Error** dashing across balding heads of **Megabazus, Lysimachus,** into arms of **Artaxerxes II** like a spider lowered inside a desert tomb, red necropolis beneath the Palace of Darius.

>Bodies of the murdered blown into forgetfulness, the pollen of posies, her laughter.

>**Error** walking across ceiling towards **Saturn**, moon gulped above the temple doorway.

>Men making love amongst canals of wine, a sickle in right hand dragged across the face of prettified dead. **Eunuch III** handed the beating heart of his master.

>**Error** laughing into black air, everlasting. A dice tumbled from heaven. The night is chance.

Vassilczenkoi

Nightmares come in dreams
        When the Apollo 17
Landed for a final time
And the crew saw their own bodies
Duplicate in a convex mirror.
Commander Eugene Cernan
Crying in his tinfoil chamber
Reawakens on Gemini 9A.
A single tear fallen,
Follows the orbit of a hand
Like a small star,
Eats the whole of Albuquerque
into Silver City, New Mexico.
A woman asleep in a hospice
        in Minnesota
Dreaming of helium-3.

Motion sickness guided them
Past their own fertility
Into the low pulse of their
        small bones.
A body splintered apart
Inside an ordinary bucket,
The reflection of a hypothesis
Caught in its frozen eye.

Mercury has no moons.
        It drifts.

Elymaitica

Roofs tiled with blue and green chalk,
Men carrying blocks of cement like orange lungs
Filled with long wires of iron
That drew and revealed their exile.
Breath of a worried computer
Rushed the palace door!

"An unknown city beneath Kalamazoo, Michigan," it calculated.
It multiplied. It subtracted.
Because it always made sense of what felt unknown.
Blue moon coming through the window
And the glow you see in plasma around an object.

      They call it St. Elmo's fire.

The coffin of their master, launched into space
                  as an administrative error.

A kiss like a line drawn across the mute red circle,
Staggered backwards against the brick wall.

Minotaur.

Irinae

Limousines like solar storms
Covered in sickness
            moved through a shape.
Wolves driving from Bel Air
To the end of August
To the entrance of a house.
            A magician in Switzerland
                    In August 1898.

She paid the staff
As though they knew
            That time reveals nothing
other than its own patience.
The chauffeur swallowed an entire atom
And turned the wheel.
Summer like a stutter
            From the beak of a nightjar
Burst into fire.
            Blue peninsula blooming
White monkey flowers, sphinx moths
pouring downwards.

            Klazomenian sarcophagi
                    Nailed to the door.

CHORUS:

O ERROR//

EXILED FROM ABOVE//

TEMPTATION OF EVEN THE PUREST//

LET US REACH THY TEMPLE//

OF WONDERFUL MISFORTUNE//

LET US SURRENDER TO WICKEDNESS//

VENGEFUL AND PETTY GODS//

THAT DECIDE OUR LIVES//

WITH LITTLE THOUGHT OR CARE//

WE WISH TO RUN AS FAST AS YOU//

SO WE MIGHT ESCAPE//

RUN WITH THE FOOLISH DEAD//

INTO MEADOWS OF STUPIDITY//

A SOLDIER THAT TURNS HIS BACK ON LIFE//

TO FACE A DAFFODIL//

Coziae

Look upon our many tumours
        Like sweetness,
Laurels placed upon
        the heads of men
Made king by an infection.
        A pact with Tengri–
Gods littered with bacteria,
Wealth of sickness,
        Its corpse risen again,
In bunches of sweet rocket
And catmint,
Where the Black Sea meets
        The Sea of Azov.

Eunuch III

Fountain

Candelabra

Error

Xanthina

Brazil backwards
Falling down an escalator.
Blue flies crawling
Across her collarbones,
She spoke of a satellite in space
Filled with snakes
          and a zu bird.

Images on the computer screen
Of Edom on fire
          Transmitted
Shown in
          orange-yellow-blue-green.
She spoke of becoming night
In the internet cafe.

When darkness fell
She took a knife and dragged
It across the glass.
          A sidereal day caught
Above the palm
Of a common *puta*
Emerged from the green.

          Jophiel,
          archangel of beauty,
Teleports into Molniya orbit,
Mouth spilling with space debris,
Body blistered in vanity,
          Hot like a chicken carcass
Dragged into the sky.

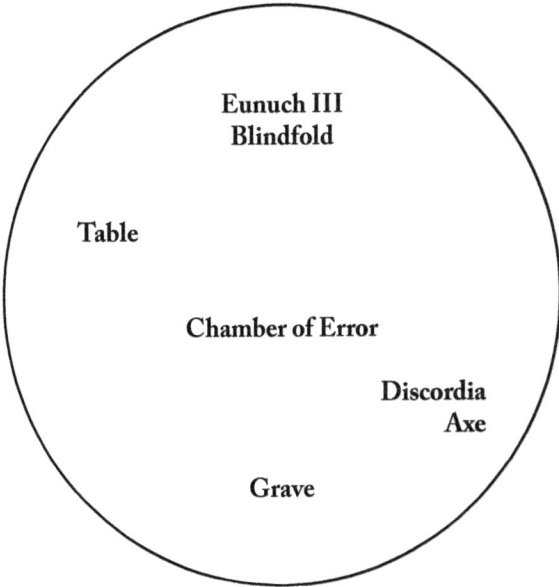

Eunuch III
Blindfold

Table

Chamber of Error

Discordia
Axe

Grave

Ozcelikii

We rush north
          like dreams
Into the frozen blue…

A yellow rose
Placed at the feet
      Of a shadow…

          … Pluto.

>>**Discordia**, mother of **Error** and bringer of chaos, walks backwards through the wall<<

>>blue silk blindfold placed over the eyes of **Eunuch III** and span into innocent confusion<<

>>two crystal vials: one of deadly mandrake and other wine, each placed to his blushed cheeks<<

>>**Discordia** screaming like skeleton undone, meat unravelled from the kissing mouth<<

>>a howl as axe thrown into the air<<

>>**Eunuch III** digging through ground into own grave, finds an entrance into Tartarus—end of the world<<

>>**Discordia** led on a bed of riches, screams chase him into the ground<<

EPILOGUE: Eunuch III reaches **Tartarus,** unknown tomb sinking into endless abyss. He closes his eyes and steps forward into the banished.

Lay out your unrest

www.ingramcontent.com/pod-product-compliance
Lightning Source LLC
LaVergne TN
LVHW041235080426

835508LV00011B/1215